Fun Cat Facts for Kids 9 - 12

Fun Animal Facts for Kids Book 1

Jacquelyn Elnor Johnson

www.CrimsonHillBooks.com

© 2016, 2021, 2024 Crimson Hill Books/Crimson Hill Products Inc.

All rights reserved worldwide. No part of this book, including words and illustrations, maybe be copied, lent for publication, excerpted, licensed, quoted nor used for artificial intelligence (AI) training. No robots nor any other form of AI were involved in any aspect of creating this work.

First edition, October 2016.
Second edition, January 2021.
Third edition, January 2024.

Cataloguing in Publication Data

Pulsifer, Tristan | Johnson, Jacquelyn Elnor

Fun Cat Facts for Kids 9-12

Description: Crimson Hill Books trade paperback edition | Nova Scotia, Canada

ISBN: 978-1-990291-32-6 (Paperback - Ingram)

BISAC: JNF003040 Juvenile Nonfiction: Animals - Cats
JNF003170 Juvenile Nonfiction: Animals - Pets
JNF051150 Juvenile Nonfiction: Science & Nature – Zoology

THEMA: WNGC - Cats as pets
YNNJ22 - Children's / Teenage general interest: Cats
YNNH2 - Children's / Teenage general interest: Pets & pet care: cats

Record available at https://www.bac-lac.gc.ca/eng/Pages/home.aspx

Book design: Jesse Johnson

Crimson Hill Books
(a division of)
Crimson Hill Products Inc.
Wolfville, Nova Scotia
Canada

We are pet owners, not veterinarians. Nothing included in this book is meant to serve as medical advice. If you suspect your pet is ill, please see your local vet. We accept no liability concerning your pet ownership.

A happy Siamese cat.

A mother cat with her kitten.

Cats are the only animal that chose to live with people

There are many animals that people domesticated. (Here's how to say this word: DOH-mess-ti-kate-ted).

Domesticated means people started using these animals to do work or for food. For example, people tamed horses to ride on or pull wagons. Dogs were tamed to do jobs like be watchdogs, carry supplies or pull sleds.

Before cats or dogs were pets, they did jobs for people.

Other animals became food for people. We use goats and cows to get milk, both these animals and pigs for meat and chickens for eggs. None of these animals chose to serve people. They would rather be wild and live their natural lives without humans.

Only cats chose to live with people and serve as mousers. This means the cats caught and ate mice and rats.

Cats didn't do this simply to make the people happy.

People didn't want mice and rats in their homes or barns. Rodents (mice and rats) eat grain and other foods and carry germs that cause diseases. These diseases can make people seriously ill.

Cats protected the food crops (like wheat, oats and barley).

Cats also helped protect farm animals and people from sicknesses spread by mice or rats.

People were delighted. It was also good for the cats. Cats are meat-eaters. Their ideal meal is a mouse or a small rat.

Very long ago, wild dogs chose to live near people, because dogs found discarded food and bones that people left in their garbage heaps.

Eventually, people tamed some dogs to work for people or live with them.

Only cats chose to move in with people and share their homes, starting about 10,000 years ago.

Millions of people, and millions of pet cats around the world are happy that they did.

Cats have excellent balance.

When did cats first appear on earth?

Both cats and dogs come from the same ancient ancestor, an animal called the miacid that vanished long ago.

Scientists believe that cats first appeared about 11 million years ago, probably in a rain forest somewhere in Asia.

The first time cats appeared in human writing was in Egyptian hieroglyphs that were written on walls about 4,000 years ago.

Hieroglyphs are pictures that represent words. So, we know that people in Egypt had a word for "cat" 4,000 years ago and possibly even earlier than this.

This is an ocelot.

Did the native North American people have pet cats?

No, they didn't. There weren't any pet cats in North America until not very long ago. But there were wild cats in the forests and mountains, and have been for a very long time.

Millions of years ago, there were several kinds of sabre-tooth cats in North America. These fierce cats died out thousands of years ago.

Today, there are five types of wild cats that live in what is now Mexico, United States and Canada. They are: lynx, bobcat, ocelot, cougar (also known as the puma or mountain lion) and jaguar. The jaguar is the largest. It is also the only cat in North America that knows how to roar.

All these wild cats live in remote places. They avoid people, so we rarely see them.

The North American native peoples knew about these wild cats, but did not have pet cats.

There were no pet cats anywhere in North America until about 260 years ago.

That's when the first cats arrived from Europe and Britain. They came on ships with British and European people who wanted to trade or settle in what they called the New World.

On these ships, the cats weren't pets. They had the job of keeping mice and rats from eating the grain and other food stored onboard.

Both the people and their horses and farm animals relied on the cats to protect their food supply. Without the ship cats helping to protect their food, they might not have made it safely. They might have run out of food before they reached land.

Some of these people made their new home in North America. Others settled in Central America, South America, South Africa, Australia and New Zealand.

In all these places, cats arrived with the settlers. Cats were happy living with people because people gave them warm, safe places to live. Cats became very comfortable living with people.

Today, there are millions of pet cats and feral cats in North America. Feral means cats that are wild. Feral cats usually live near people, but not with them.

Almost all of today's pet and feral cats in North America, South America, Central America, Australia, New Zealand and South Africa are the great-great-

A Canadian Lynx.

great-great-grandcats of those first cats who came on ships of explorers and settlers from Britain and Europe in the 1600s and 1700s.

Cats with feet like snowshoes

The Canada lynx is an animal people seldom see, so there are many things we don't know about this mysterious animal.

Things we do know about this animal are:

- They are about twice as big as the average pet cat.
- They have no tail, so they probably don't jump like other cats do.
- They have super sensitive hearing (even for a cat!)
- They have very thick fur.
- They can only lose heat from their nose, ears or eyes.
- Their feet don't sweat, like other cats.

It is a Canada lynx's feet that are truly remarkable. They have huge paws, shaped like snowshoes.

Their big feet allow them to run as fast as 30 miles per hours (48 km/h) on snow. That's about 15 times faster than a healthy person can travel, wearing lightweight modern snowshoes.

Cat Fun Fact:

Humans would be poisoned if they drink seawater. That's not true for cats. They'd always rather have cold, fresh water. They can drink saltwater if they have to and it won't hurt them.

A cat's eyes are different and so they see things differently then we do.

Do cats see better than people?

When you can't find something, has anyone ever said to you, "It's right under your nose?" It's a common expression.

What they mean when they say this is the thing you're looking for is right in front of you. You can't miss seeing it, unless your eyes are closed.

But here's a funny thing about cats. They *can't* see anything that's right under their nose! This is because of the way their eyes are positioned on their faces. If you put a treat right under a cat's nose, it would smell that treat and want it, but your cat couldn't see it!

(Be careful not to tease your cat by doing this for more than a moment. Cats pounce on food and you could get bitten!)

Cats aren't colour-blind, but they don't see colours the way people do. We don't know a lot about how well cats can see, but we know for certain that they can see blue, green and red. Probably, when they do see these colours, they aren't as bright as they appear to most people.

There are two ways that cats see very much better than people. One is that cats have wider peripheral vision. (Say this long word like this: PURR-if-fur-all). Peripheral means seeing not just what is in front of you, but also what is at the sides of your head.

How good is your peripheral vision?

Try this. Look at something straight ahead of you. Put your hands in front of your face, then slowly move your right hand towards your right ear and your left hand towards your left ear. When do your hands 'disappear?' When they do, that is called the limit or edge of your peripheral vision.

Cats also have much better night vision than people do. They can see six times better than people can when it is almost dark. Like people, cats can't see anything when it is totally dark.

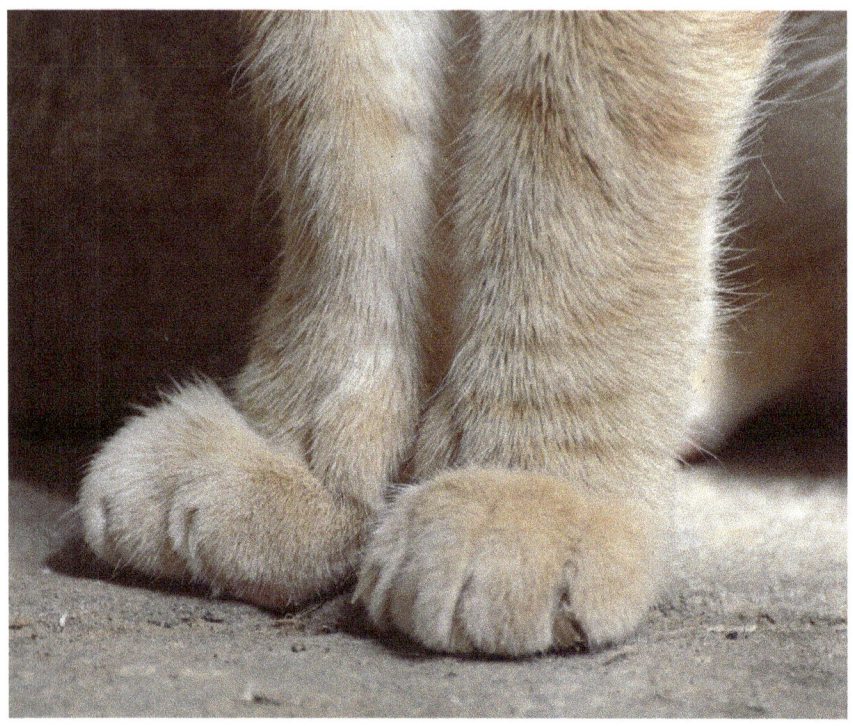

Do cats walk on their toes?

Cats' paws and claws are their toes, so the answer to this question is, "Yes."

No one knows when or why cats first started walking on their toes instead of their feet, like all other mammals do.

Mammal is the name for the huge family of animals that includes dogs, horses, bears, lions, whales, gorillas, seals, tigers, elephants and many other living creatures, including people.

Maybe cats walk on their toes because it makes it easier to climb? Or it could just be more comfortable for them?

This is a blue spotted tabby cat.

Why do cats have tails?

Have you ever wondered why cats have tails? What is a tail used for, or is their tail just so they look good?

The answer is cats' tails aren't just attractive. They are also useful. Without a tail, a cat wouldn't be nearly as good at jumping.

Cats are very good at jumping and landing exactly where they want to land.

They can do this partly because they have a strong spine (a spine is a backbone) and powerful back and leg muscles. When they jump, their tails help them keep their balance.

Cat Fun Fact:
Cats can only sweat through their paws.

A young Siamese cat.

What is so strange about white cats?

There are several strange things about white cats.

One is that all Siamese kittens are born white. As their baby fluff turns into fur, it becomes the tan and brown coat of an adult Siamese cat. But this won't happen if the Siamese kittens live in a very hot place (more than 98 degrees F. or 36.6 degrees C.).

Siamese cats have albino genes that only work in very warm rooms.

When this happens, the kittens will never develop the darker brown ears, legs and tail that Siamese cats are known for. They will stay a pure creamy white colour.

This adult cat has beautiful eyes.

A white mother cat can have kittens that are any colour – gray, black, tortoiseshell or ginger.

White cats that have bare skin on their ears can suffer sunburn very easily, just like people with very fair, sensitive skin.

White cats that have blue eyes are almost always deaf. (Deaf means they can't hear.)

If a white cat has one blue eye and one green eye, the ear that is on the same side as the blue eye will be deaf.

White cats with orange eyes have normal hearing.

Another strange fact about cats' paws

All female cats are right-pawed. Most male cats are left-pawed.

Being right-pawed or left-pawed is like being right-handed or left-handed for people.

If you are right-handed, as most people are, you naturally do most tasks with your right hand, such as brushing your hair or cursive writing.

In humans, about 1 out of every 10 people is left-handed and about 1 out of every 100 people can use either hand equally well.

Left-handedness happens more often in boys than in girls.

Why do cats like meat? Can cats eat other things?

Unlike dogs, or people, cats must have meat. That's almost the only thing they can eat and want to eat.

Cats can't eat vegetables, nuts, seeds or grains.

They are not able to taste sugar, or anything sweet. Anything with sugar in it is very unhealthy for a cat to eat.

They also should never be given people food or dog food. If you feed your cat nothing but dog food, he or she will become blind because there is no taurine in dog food. Cats must have taurine for healthy eyes and teeth. Taurine is in meat, chicken, shrimp and shellfish.

Fun Cat Facts for Kids 9 - 12

Cats live on meat, poultry and fish. But they can also eat a little bit of some fruits. Fruits that are safe for cats to eat a little bit of are:

- bananas
- apples
- pears
- mangos
- pineapple
- blueberries
- watermelon
- cantaloupe.

Some fruits are dangerous for cats to eat, because these could make them very sick and damage their kidneys.

Fruits to <u>never</u> feed your cat are grapes, raisins, oranges, lemons, limes, grapefruit and tangerines.

If you do give your cat fruit, first you need to wash the fruit carefully. Peel the fruit and cut out the seeds, pits and rinds.

Cut the fruit into bite-sized pieces before you give it to your cat.

Sometimes, cats eat grass or leaves from houseplants. They do this because they have an upset stomach and their body is telling them that they need to throw up.

Any food you give your cat needs to be cut into small chunks. Cats can't chew their food. Sometimes, they swallow food that is too big. This is dangerous because they could choke. Or they must vomit (throw up) to get rid of it.

Do cats eat insects?

Most pet cats enjoy trying to catch any small thing that moves, including houseflies and other small flying insects. Sometimes, they eat them.

But there is one type of cat that specializes in eating insects. It is the Rusty spotted cat. This little orange cat lives in Sri Lanka, in Asia. Its favourite food is locusts, a type of grasshopper.

This sand cat lives in a zoo.

World's hottest cats

Sand cats, also called Sand dune cats, are another wild cat that humans seldom see. They live in desert areas of North Africa, the Middle East countries and Central Asia.

These hot, dry places can get to be 117 degrees F. (47 degrees C.). This is far too hot for humans to be able to survive. But sand cats have developed so they can.

They are excellent diggers. They dig burrows to live in because it's a bit cooler underground.

A Bengal cat and her kittens.

They usually sleep during the hottest part of the day, and come out to hunt early in the morning or late in the evening. They eat small snakes, birds, desert gerbils and insects.

There are two very strange things about desert cats. One is that they can meow and purr, just like most cats. But they can make a lot of other sounds. Strangest of all, they can bark like a dog! Their bark sounds just like a Chihuahua's bark!

They have also developed a way to walk on hot sand without hurting their paws. A sand cat's paws are covered in thick fur to protect their feet.

Though sand cat kittens are just as adorable as any other type of kitten, they can never be pets. Sand cats insist on living alone. They do everything they can to avoid people.

This is a carving of Bastet.

Did ancient Egyptians worship cats?

Ancient Egyptians believed that animals are creatures that live half way between the world of people and the world of the gods.

For this reason, they often turned birds and animals into mummies after they died and buried them in a ceremony, like a funeral for humans.

A mummy is the preserved body of a person, or animal, that is dead. The body is treated with herbs and then wrapped in cotton and put into a wood box, then into a stone tomb.

One of the important Egyptian goddesses was Bastet, who people thought looked like she was a woman with a head like a cat.

Originally, Bastet had a lioness, but then she was changed to be a cat goddess and the goddess of the moon.

Cats got a lot of respect in ancient Egypt. Killing a cat was a major crime. When a family's pet cat died, everyone in that family shaved their eyebrows as a sign of mourning. Ancient Egyptians believed that cats are the guardians, or protectors, of the dead.

One of Egypt's enemies used this ancient Egyptian love of cats to try to defeat them. During a war with Persia, the Egyptians were winning. Then a Persian general had an idea. He captured hundreds of cats and then released them all on the battlefield.

When the Egyptian general saw this, he surrendered. It was the only way to be sure none of the cats were hurt.

What did ancient Egyptian cats look like?

Egypts's cats in ancient times had long bodies, tails, legs and faces. Their fur was short and could be spotted or striped, like modern tabby cats.

Can cats be heroes?

There are many stories about cats who saved their owners' lives.

One of these stories is about Meskie. One evening, her owner fell asleep watching TV. Suddenly, Meskie jumped onto her owner's lap, waking her up and acting very strangely.

Meskie insisted that her owner follow her to the kitchen. It was on fire! The owner called for help, grabbed her car keys and Meskie and rushed out of her burning house.

Firefighters couldn't save their home, but Meskie and her owner survived because Meskie, the hero cat, woke up in time for them to escape.

Gepetto is usually a quiet cat. Then one winter night, his owner woke up with a headache, turned over and went back to sleep. But soon, Gepetto's yowling woke her up again. She felt even worse, really sick now, like she had the flu, but she went to see what was wrong.

For some reason, Gepetto was making a lot of noise, sitting at the top of the stairs. He insisted that they go down to the basement. His owner didn't want to do this, in the middle of the night! It was dark down there and cold. She felt sick now and just wanted to sleep.

Fortunately, this cat owner didn't just go back to bed. She called her husband, who was at work and told him about what was going on.

She said she had a terrible headache, felt very odd and dizzy. And their cat was saying something was wrong in the basement.

They are also very fortunate that the husband knew exactly what was wrong.

"Get out of the house immediately!" he said. "Right now! Go!"

What the husband thought might be happening turned out to be true. Their house had filled up with carbon monoxide, a deadly poison gas.

The owner couldn't smell it, but Gepetto could!

The owner went to hospital, where doctors said that Gepetto had saved her life.

If she'd stayed at home that day and just gone back to bed, like she wanted to do, ignoring Gepetto's cries about the danger, they both would have died.

Gas leaks in houses are very rare. But when this happens, hero pets can raise the alarm!

Fun Cat Facts for Kids 9 - 12

Melzy was adopted from an animal shelter. Her owner is Alex, who is 9 years old and has diabetes. One night when Alex was sleeping, Melzy climbed up the ladder to his loft bed, something she'd never done before.

She swatted Alex with her paws until he got up. This was also very unusual.

Then she walked him downstairs to the kitchen, where his sugar testing kit is.

If you have diabetes or know someone like Alex, you know you always need to do this test, sometimes several times a day. The test tells what your blood sugar level is. You want it to always be normal.

If your sugar level gets too low, you could become seriously ill fast and need to go to Emergency (A&E).

Alex and his mother did the test. They were amazed to find that Melzy was right!

Alex's sugar level was dangerously low, even though he didn't feel dizzy or have any of the other signs of low blood sugar that people with diabetes always watch out for.

All Alex needed to do was drink some fruit juice. But Melzy insisted that he check his blood sugar one more time before he went back to bed.

Soon Alex was OK again and ready to go back to sleep.

But if Melzy hadn't noticed something was wrong and woken Alex and his Mum up in the middle of the night, he might not have survived.

Their whole family is proud of Melzy, their hero cat!

How did Melzy know Alex's blood sugar level was low? Do you know the answer?

Here's how. The smell of Alex's breath changed, just a bit, when he was in trouble. People wouldn't be able to notice this, but cats, with their super-sniffers, can.

Cat Fun Fact:

In the entire world there are more than 500 million pet cats.

These are Singapura cats.

What is the smallest cat in the world?

There are about 100 breeds of pet cats in the world today.

The smallest cat breed is the Singapura. It usually weighs less than half as much as other pet cats, or about 4 pounds (1.8 kg)

But the smallest cat ever known to live was tiny. His name was Mr. Pebbles and he weighed just 3 pounds (1.3 kg). He was only 2 ¾ inches (7 cm) tall and 7 ½ inches (19 cm) long.

The largest breed of pet cats is the Maine Coon cat, weighing more than twice as much as most healthy

pet cats, or 25 pounds (11.6 kg). The Ragdoll breed is almost as large.

The heaviest known cat was Himmy, who lived in Queensland, Australia. He weighed nearly 47 pounds (21 kg)! Sadly, because he was so overweight, he wasn't healthy. He died when he was only 10 years old, which is still young for a cat.

If you have a cat that is too fat, ask your veterinarian how to help your cat get back to a healthy weight so he or she can feel better and live longer.

Cat Fun Fact:
One year in a cat's life is the same as 15 years in a human's life.

Do cats really have 9 lives?

Cats are very good at staying alive. Maybe this is why there's an old saying that all cats have 9 lives.

They don't really. It's just an old saying.

How old can cats get?

Feral (wild) cats have short lives. Most of them live for only a few years. Life in the wild is hard for them.

Pet cats that are outdoor cats usually live for about 11 to 13 years. There are many dangers for them outside, including:

- fighting with other cats or dogs
- poisons like weed-killer used to help lawns and garden plants grow
- wild creatures that carry diseases such as mice and squirrels
- being stung by a bee.

But the most dangerous of all is being hit by a car.

Because they are protected from all these dangers, indoor cats can live much longer. With good food, good care and visits to the vet for their shots and when they're ill, indoor cats usually live 15 to 20 years or more.

These days, it isn't unusual to hear about a cat in his or her 20s.

Rarely, cats live even longer than that. Cream Puff, who lived with a family in Texas, was 38 years old when she died in 2005.

Very young kittens can fit in the palm of your hand.

'Fraidy cats

Have you ever called someone a " 'fraidy cat?" Or been called one?

It's an expression used for someone who is very shy, or scared of doing something they've never done before, like diving into a pool. It's not kind to call someone a 'fraidy cat, because that's name-calling.

No one likes to be called names.

But where did this idea of cats being afraid really come from?

No one can say for sure. Perhaps it's because cats would always rather run away from danger or a big mistake, like knocking over a lamp that breaks.

When something like this happens, your cat thinks that if he isn't there, then it wasn't his fault and maybe it didn't happen! Cats aren't good at taking responsibility for bad behaviour (neither are dogs).

What is fight or flight?

This isn't cats being bad on purpose. They're just being – cats! This is the way their brains work. We call this the "fight or flight" response, and humans do it, too. What this means is that when there's a threat or a problem, you either fight it, or get out of there fast!

Fight or flight makes sense, as the way to stay alive. This has been true for so long that it is an instinct, both for animals and for people.

It might be that people called cats " 'fraidy cats" because cats have a very fast heartbeat. In humans, when you're afraid, your heart beats a lot faster.

The normal heartbeat for a cat is 140 to 220 beats per minute. For people it is 60 to 100 beats per minute. So, a cat's normal heartbeat is about twice as fast as a human's heartbeat.

Cats are one of the few animals that aren't afraid of heights, but they usually hide when there's danger. Maybe being a 'fraidy cat is just being smart and careful, so you can have 9 lives...or one very good and long life.

What do you think?

Do cats have 9 lives?

What if people had 9 lives? Would that be good? Why?

Is only half of this cat unlucky?

Are black cats lucky or unlucky?

Thinking that something brings good luck or bad luck is a superstition. This means it isn't true; it's just a belief people have.

Here are some common superstitions:

1. If you break a mirror, you will have seven years of bad luck
2. Don't open your umbrella until you get outside, or put a hat on your bed, or walk under a ladder. These will all bring bad luck.
3. But you could get some good luck if you find a coin on the ground and pick it up.
4. If you give someone a purse, wallet or handbag as a gift, put a coin in it. This will give them good luck.

5. Finding a four-leaf clover, making a wish on a chicken's or turkey's wishbone or making a wish on a shooting star can all bring good luck.

In some places in the world, black cats are thought to bring lots of good luck. This is true in Great Britain, for example. In Scotland, people believe that if a black cat comes to your home, your family will be blessed.

Sailors thought that the ship's cat should be black, to bring them back to land safely. But if a black cat walked onto a ship, and then right off that ship, they believed that ship would sink on its next voyage! Sailors were very superstitious!

Today in most of Europe, United States and some parts of Canada, many people think that black pets, especially black dogs or cats, are unlucky.

So where did this odd idea about cats that are black being lucky, or unlucky, come from?

No one really knows.

What do you think?

Are black cats lucky? Are they unlucky?

Or are they just like any other cat, except they have black fur?

A mother cat and kitten.

Do cats always land on their feet?

Cats try to always land on their feet. They do this so that they won't injure their backs. They'd rather have their strongest body part – their legs – under them.

If a cat falls, it will turn in mid-air so that it lands feet-first.

If a person fell from the twentieth floor of a building, they probably wouldn't survive.

But if a cat fell from the same place, it could survive.

To understand this, we need to do some math.

The twentieth floor of a building is about 200 feet or 61 meters above the ground.

Objects fall at 32 feet per second (or 9.75 meters per second).

A cat needs to fall about eight floors, or 80 feet (or almost 24 and a half meters) to do what is called cat-righting.

Here's what the cat must do:

   1. realize what is happening,

   2. relax,

   3. correct their body position in mid-air, so their paws are down.

And they land on their feet.

The amazing thing is any cat can right himself or herself in just two and a half seconds! Cats don't learn how to do this, they are born knowing how to do this.

No other animal has this strange ability.

A cat that falls from a place closer to the ground – say only four storeys up in the air or 40 feet (12 meters) – doesn't have enough time to right himself or herself. They can't land on their feet. They could be seriously hurt.

Cat Fun Fact:

There were no pet cats in North America until European settlers brought them to United States in 1750. These new cat immigrants didn't come to be lap cats. They were put to work right away as mouse catchers.

How high can a cat jump?

Cats are brilliant jumpers, far better than almost any other animal or human. From sitting still, a cat can jump straight up in the air to a height of 7 times his own height. No human can do this.

This would be like you sitting on the floor and suddenly jumping as high as two school busses – one stacked on top of the other!

How are cats able to do this incredible feat? It's because of their bodies. They have strong back and leg muscles and a very flexible spine (or backbone). They also don't weigh a lot, compared to their size and muscle strength.

Because they need to leap or move quickly to pounce on the birds, fish and other creatures they eat (when they're wild) cats evolved to be tremendous jumpers!

Fun Cat Facts for Kids 9 - 12

Evolved means that over thousands and thousands of years, cats gradually changed. They got lighter, faster and better at doing everything necessary to catch their food.

That's why the cats of today are such fantastic jumpers. They're also very good climbers. Unfortunately, cats can't come back down from the high places they climb up to very well. Their claws are turned for climbing up, not climbing down face-first.

Feral cat mothers teach their kittens many things, including how to climb back down from a tree.

But outdoor cats that didn't learn this when they were kittens can get up a tree and not know how to get down again. They might jump down, or wait to be rescued.

Are cats allergic to milk and cream?

How often have you seen a photo of someone giving a cat milk or cream to lap up?

Or maybe you give your pet milk all the time?

Lots of people do, because cats seem to like milk. Unfortunately, milk makes them ill. The reason is that, except for their own mother's milk when they are new kittens, most cats can't digest cow milk. They are allergic to milk, just like people who are lactose-intolerant.

Milk gives them a terrible stomach ache and diarrhea.

Don't give your cat these!

Here are some other things you might have in your home or your garage, yard or garden that are dangerous for cats to eat:

- Chocolate or any food with caffeine in it, like coffee, tea and soda pop.
- Gum or candy. It usually has a chemical in it called Xylitol that is poison to cats.
- Any medicine meant for humans. Aspirin is especially dangerous.
- Wine, beer, or anything with alcohol in it.
- Plants that are poison for cats and most other pets are azaleas, mums, lilies, tulips, rhododendrons, mistletoe, poinsettias and marijuana.
- Bleach and other cleaning supplies.

- Antifreeze and gardening chemicals, such as weed-killer.
- Tap water. If you live in a city or town, the water that comes out of your taps probably has chlorine in it.

Chlorine is a chemical used to clean the water, but it can burn a cat's nose. Unless your family's water comes from a well, give your pets spring water, or bottled water.

Or pour some tap water in a bowl and let it sit for 24 hours before you give it to your pet.

This is long enough for all the chorine in the water to evaporate into the air. (say this word like this: Eee-VAP-pour-rate). Evaporate means leave the water and go up into the air.

If your cat has breathing problems, is coughing, is suddenly very confused, vomiting, has diarrhea, is shivering, has tremors or seizures, or seems very weak or has a skin rash, she might have swallowed something that is poisonous for cats.

You need to call your vet right away!

Be sure to keep their number close to the phone or where you can easily find it quickly in an emergency.

Do cats sweat?

Cats who live in places that are cold in winter, but warm in summer have a thick winter coat with a top layer and an undercoat.

In spring, they shed part of this coat so they'll be a bit cooler in the summer months. This is why, when you have pet cats and live in a place where there is sometimes cold weather, you will have to clean up the cat hair. This is easy to do. Just brush it off soft furniture, dust other furniture, and use a vacuum cleaner on the floors.

Cats can sweat to cool off, but not the way people do. Cats sweat only through the bottom of their paws!

In warm weather, cats need other ways to cool off, including more cool water to drink and shady or cool places to nap.

Why do cats have whiskers?

Cats don't have a collar bone. Their shoulder bones connect to muscle, not bone.

This means that the widest part of their body isn't their shoulders. It's their head. But in order to tell if a door is wide enough for them to walk through (this really means wide enough to get their head through) they need a way to measure.

That's one of the jobs of a cat's whiskers. It tells the cat how wide a space is that they want to walk through. Cats 'mind the gap' with their whiskers!

Whiskers also are amazing sensors. The wild Fishing Cats that live in Sri Lanka, in Asia, are a cat that likes water. Even when the water is too muddy to see anything, a Fisher Cat can dip her whiskers into the water and sense exactly where a fish is so she can catch it for dinner!

This is a tuxedo cat. Tuxedos, also called a black-and-white are natural acrobats.

Why are some people allergic to cats?

Some people are allergic to cat dander, which is little flakes of dry skin. Or they might be allergic to something in cats' saliva.

If you are allergic to cats, when you're around them your eyes water, you start to sneeze and feel like you're getting a cold. To feel better, you could take an allergy pill. Or just go somewhere where there aren't any cats.

This is a hairless cat breed called the sphynx.

Female cats are less likely to cause problems for people with a cat allergy than male cats.

If you have a cat allergy, you might be OK with just one female cat.

Another answer is to get a hairless cat. Hairless cats are a special breed of cat that is completely bald! They are called sphynx cats.

They are a bit funny looking, but people with a cat allergy can usually have a hairless pet and have no allergy problem.

Why do cats like women better than men?

Some cats seem to prefer children and women, but not like men very much. This could be because children and women talk with a higher-pitched voice than most men do.

Cats have hearing that is much better than human hearing. They can hear sounds we can't hear.

One of those very high-pitched sounds cats can hear easily (but we can't) is the squeaking sound mice make when they 'talk' to each other.

If you think your cat wants to hear higher-pitched voices, try talking in a higher-pitched voice to your cat and see what happens.

Cats' super hearing ability

It also means that you shouldn't talk loudly or make loud noises very close to your cat's ears, like putting your face close to theirs and shouting at them.

The cat won't care what you're saying. It will care that the loud sound is causing pain in their head.

Cats can also hear sounds that are not close to their ears. They can hear a sound clearly that would be too far away for people to hear. Their excellent hearing means they hear sounds from four or five times further away than people can hear!

Cats often try to hide when there is a loud noise, like running the vacuum cleaner. They aren't afraid of the machine. They just really don't like the noise!

Why do cats sleep so much?

All mammals, including cats and people, need to get enough good sleep.

Sleep is the time when our bodies fight off infection or illness, repair cuts or any other wounds and when our bodies grow.

Newborn kittens sleep almost all the time. Sleep is the only time their bodies produce growth hormones. Since they need to grow quickly, they need to sleep a lot!

Healthy adult pet cats sleep deeply for only about 3 ½ hours a day. But they take catnaps for another 12 hours or so each day. This means they're only awake for about 7 or 8 hours a day!

Everything is better after a good yawn.

But the real champion catnapers are male lions. They sleep for 20 hours a day, leaving all the work of hunting and family life to the lady lions, called lionesses.

And here's another interesting fact about sleeping cats. They can wake up instantly from deep sleep when they hear a sound that might mean danger. No other animal can do this, and neither can people!

This is a Cheetah.

How fast can a cat run?

Pet cats don't ever run for very long. They run in short spurts of energy. But when they do decide to run, they can reach the speed of 31 mph (49 kph). That's faster than the world's fastest human runner. Usain Bolt's top time is 28 mph (45 kph).

But that's not even half as fast as the world's fastest cat can run. Cheetahs have been timed running 70 mph (112.6 kph).

Fun Cat Facts for Kids 9 - 12

Their flexible spines and long muscles are what allow cats to run so fast. However, they don't run for long because they get tired very quickly, sometimes allowing the animals they are chasing to escape.

Why does a cat have a rough tongue?

A cat's tongue isn't smooth like a person's tongue. Instead, cats have a lot of tiny hooks all over their tongues. These hooks help them clean their fur. Cats are very picky about keeping themselves clean.

But the problem they have is when they lick their fur and paws to clean them, or groom another cat they live with, cats also swallow hair. This forms into hairballs. Cats have strong acid in their stomachs to help them digest their food, but this acid can't digest hair. A cat has to throw up when he or she has hairballs.

If your cat has a lot of hairballs, they need you to brush their fur gently. This works the same as brushing your hair to get rid of the dead hairs and

This is a Ragdoll kitten.

keep your scalp healthy. Your scalp is the skin under your hair.

Cats with long hair, like Main Coon cats or Ragdoll cats, need to be brushed every day. Smooth-haired cats, like a tortoiseshell, tuxedo or ginger cat, need to be brushed two times a week.

Cats don't like baths. If you do have to bathe your cat, don't use shampoo or soap that is for people. It will not be good for their skin or their coat. You can find cat shampoo at any pet store and many online pet supply stores.

This cat has strong, healthy teeth.

Cat teeth

How are a cat's teeth like a human's teeth?

Cats are biters because that's how they catch and kill their food.

Kittens have 26 baby teeth, but they lose their baby teeth when they're about 6 months old. That's when their adult teeth grow in.

Adult cats have 30 teeth.

Children also lose their baby teeth, but not until they're about eight years old.

This is a Mieze cat.

What do cats share with only two other creatures on earth?

Let's see if you can guess the answer to this question?

Here's a hint: the two other creatures that also do this are camels and giraffes.

Here's the answer: it's the strange way they walk. It is completely different to every other four-footed animal. Camels, giraffes and cats all step with both right legs, then both left legs.

***Cat Fun Fact:**
A group of adult cats is called a clowder. A group of kittens is called a kindle.*

Where in the world do cats have six toes?

Almost everywhere in the world, pet cats and feral cats usually have five toes on their front paws and four toes on their back paws. So, 18 toes altogether.

But sometimes, a cat is born with extra toes. They might have as many as seven front toes. Their back paws could also have extra toes.

When this happens, the kitten with extra toes is considered to be a bit odd.

But not in the city of Boston in United States. There, six-toed cats are so common that many people are surprised when a cat with only five toes is born.

Why this can happen is called mutation (say it like this – MEUW-tay-shun).

Mutation is when a creature changes slightly. Usually, mutations happen to help creatures survive or adapt to a changing world. But sometimes they are just strange accidents.

When a mutation helps animals survive more easily, more will be born with this mutation.

What happened in Boston is that a few cats were born with six toes. These cats were very successful in having lots of kittens.

Those kittens grew up to be cats who were also very successful in living long enough to have lots of kittens.

This happened many times, until almost all the cats were the six-toed kind.

What is a kindle of cats?

When you have a group of birds of animals together in one place, you could just say there's a lot of that creature.

But in English groups of animals have their own name, depending on what the bird or animal is. Some of these names are pretty amazing!

So, for example, a group of feral cats is called a destruction of cats.

Crows sitting in a tree are a murder of crows.

Here's one you've probably heard of: a colony of ants. Or a herd of buffalo. A pod of dolphins.

But did you know about a sleuth of bears?

Or a gulp of cormorants? A dole of doves? A busyness of ferrets? A flamboyance of flamingos? A mess of iguanas?

When housecats get together, they are a clowder, a pounce or a kindle of cats.

And if you have just one cat who is a female, she is a molly, or a queen. Male cats are called toms.

Cat Fun Fact:
Every cat has a nose print that's unique, just like fingerprints are for humans. No two cats have exactly the same nose print.

Have you ever seen a liger? Or a tigon?

Maybe not, because there are fewer than 100 ligers alive in the world today. There are probably even fewer tigons. This is because these cats have never lived in the wild world. They were created in zoos as an animal curiosity.

If a male lion and a female tiger have babies together, those kittens are called ligers.

If a male tiger and a female lion have babies together, their kittens are tigons.

An adult liger is usually orange, but it can be beige with only faint stripes and spots on their belly. The markings on liger's bodies can be black, dark brown or sandy brown. Male ligers might have a short mane, or no mane at all.

All adult ligers are larger than their parents and can weigh as much as 1,200 pounds or 544 kilograms! Because ligers have no hormone that stops them growing when they become adults, they keep getting bigger and bigger throughout their entire lives!

A liger named Hercules was the largest cat that has ever lived. He was an odd-looking creature. He had no mane.

Ligers have a bite force that is twice as much as tigons. They also have a huge appetite. A liger can eat 50 pounds, or almost 23 kilograms of meat in just one meal!

Tigons have a tiger father and a lioness mother. They're small, compared to other big cats, usually weighing only 200 to 500 pounds, or 90 to 227 kilograms. They have dark orange coats, dark markings and white bellies. The males have short manes.

Ligers are gentler and more easy-going than tigers, and are social, like lions. This doesn't mean they'd make good pets. Besides their huge size, they have incredible speed and strength. And like all cats, they will be aggressive when they feel threatened. That's a cat instinct.

In most countries today it is against the law for zoos, or anyone else, to breed ligers or tigons because both these man-made animals suffer many health problems.

Fun Cat Facts for Kids 9 - 12

Nepo kitties

Do you know any nepo kids? They're kids who have rich and famous parents. But did you know there are also nepo pets who are also rich and famous because their owners are?

One of them is Chip. His owner is model and actress Claudia Schiffer. Chip is in a movie with her called *Argyll*. Chip is also an author. His book is called **Blue Chip** and he has more than 8,000 followers on Instagram @Chipthecat.

Taylor Swift also has a nepo kitty, a blue-eyed ragdoll called Benjamin Button. When *Time* magazine named Taylor Person of the Year for 2023, she took Benjamin with her to the photo shoot for the story. He sat on her should for the photo they used on *Time* magazine's front cover!

Fun Cat Facts for Kids 9 - 12

If you've seen *The Princess Diaries*, you've seen Anne Hathaway's cat, a co-star in that movie and one of the four cat actors who played Fat Louie.

Choupette is another nepo kitty who is both rich and famous. When his owner, the fashion designer Karl Lagerfeld died, Choupette inherited $1.5 million!

But Choupette won't be nearly as wealthy as the dogs owned by actor and TV show host Oprah Winfrey, reported to have set aside $30 million to care for her dogs after she has died.

Cat Fun Fact:
Cats can run 30 miles per hour, or 48 kilometres per hour.

Fun Cat Facts for Kids 9 - 12

Cats in space!

Taters the cat is a star and social media sensation after a video of him chasing a laser went viral in December 2023.

So what you might be thinking. Everybody knows cats like to chase laser pointers.

The fantastic thing about this cat chasing a laser is that the video of him doing it travelled 31 million kilometres, or more than 19 million miles back to earth from a NASA mission far out in deep space. That's about 80 times as far away as a trip from earth to the moon!

Taters never left Earth, but his video did. It was filmed before the spaceship took off. It was sent back as a test to see if it could be possible, in the future, for people to communicate from that far away. Can we stream video and other data from deep space, far beyond our own solar system and possibly even

beyond our own galaxy? That's what the NASA scientists wanted to know.

Fun Cat Facts for Kids 9 - 12

Taters' NASA Deep Space Optical Communication video lasts just 15 seconds. It's the very first high-definition video sent back to earth from a spaceship that far away from earth. The video took just 101 seconds, or less than two minutes, to travel from the NASA ship to NASA's Jet Propulsion Laboratory in California. The signal was sent at 267 megabits per second.

Taters isn't the first cat star in a video in space. A hundred years ago, when TV was just being invented, a small statue of Felix the Cat, a cartoon cat, was used to test one of the first television broadcasts. The statue was placed on a turntable. If you'd had a TV back then (almost no one did) you could have switched it on to see Felix going around and around for two hours every day. People flocked to demonstrations of this fantastic new invention to see it!

But these are just images of cats. In 1963, France sent an actual cat, named Félicette to space, through her space flight lasted only five minutes. She survived her historic flight. Now there is a statue of her at the International Space University in Strasbourg, France.

Cat Fun Fact:

About 1/4 of American and British families have a pet cat. Just over one-third of Canadian families have a cat, and close to half of Australian families do, too!

How do cats always know when you're happy or sad?

Cats don't use their faces to show how they're feeling. They don't grin when they're happy or laugh when something is funny. They don't cry when they're sad or hurt or lonely.

This is why cats don't look at each other's faces to figure out what the other cat is thinking. They might recognize a few human faces, like when we smile or when we look really angry or upset. Some cat owners are convinced that their pets can read faces, but researchers are still unsure about if this is true.

But pet cats always seem to understand how their owners are feeling and can even tell when their owners are sick. How can they do this? Again, researchers don't know for sure yet, but it's probable that cats can *smell* emotions of people they live with or meet (dogs can do this, too). They can take information about humans by very slight changes in

our natural odors. Humans don't notice these differences, for example when we're just tired, or upset, or not well, but our pets can!

Fake news!

Some of these sentences are false, but some are true. Can you spot the fake news?

1. Black cats cause bad luck.

2. Cats like candy.

3. Cats have nine lives.

4. You should brush your cat's teeth once a day.

5. You should trim your cat's whiskers.

6. You should never have a cat if you have a human baby in your family because cats will jump into the baby's crib or cot and try to suck out their air, killing the baby.

7. Tooth decay is a common problem for cats.

8. It's not unusual for cats to live twice as long as dogs.

9. Cats can get cancer.

10. Cats can see in the dark.

Did you spot the fake news and what's true in this list? These are the things that are true: numbers 4, 7, 8 and 9. Everything else here is totally FALSE, except many people believe these things are true. Some of these false beliefs have been around for hundreds of years; others are more modern.

Let's look at the TRUE answers first. Cats get tooth decay just like we do and that's why tooth brushing is good for them – and for you! – to prevent cavities. Cats can get cancer, also just like people can.

Fortunately, there is medicine that can help them survive. And it's not unusual for a cat to live for 20 years, or sometimes even longer, with good care. Most dogs live for about 10 years.

It's fake news that black cats are unlucky. They're just cats, like the ones that are white or gray or orange or any other color.

Human food is bad for cats and can make them very sick.

Cats don't suck babies' breath, but even very gentle cats should never be left alone with babies or very young children because when cats think someone or something might hurt them, they might scratch or bite to defend themselves.

And you should leave their whiskers alone. They need them to help understand their world. Whiskers don't just decorate their faces; they tell a cat useful information like 'can I fit in this small space?' and maybe other things that people who do cat research haven't discovered yet.

No living creature on earth (that we know of) can use their eyes to see in total darkness. It simply isn't possible to see in NO light. Some animals (also some people) are better at seeing when there isn't very much light, including cats.

Cats are hearty creatures and are good at running away from danger or fighting when they can't. They're also really good at getting people to take care of them. Maybe that's why some people think they have nine lives. The truth is cats each get just one life, just like us.

A basket of kittens.

Thank you!

I hope you have enjoyed this book of odd, unusual and amazing fun facts about kittens and cats.

If you want to know more about cats, I've also written I Want a Kitten. My friend Tristan, who is 9 years old, helped write that book. It's all about what it's like to have a pet cat, how to choose your new pet and how to care for him or her.

Thanks for reading!

Jacquelyn

About Jacquelyn

Jacquelyn Elnor Johnson started telling stories to entertain her younger sisters, discovering in the telling what it takes to engage your audience! By age 15, she was a correspondent for the local newspaper and had written her first book. She went on to have careers in writing for and editing newspapers and magazines and teaching journalism.

A life-long pet lover, she is the bestselling author of 14 books about caring for and enjoying pets and animals, including **I Want A Bearded Dragon** and **Fun Bearded Dragon & Leopard Gecko Facts.**

In addition to writing practical, helpful and entertaining non-fiction for kids in grades 3 to 7, she writes novels including the Morley Stories series for girls ages 10 to 13.

Find more fun books at:
www.CrimsonHillBooks.com

Photo Credits

Thank you to these photographers:

Pixabay: Brigette Werner, Alexas Fotos, Jan Mallander, Eszter Miller, Andreas Lischka, Noly, Gorks, Scott Payne, Choemik, Sarah Richter, Karin Laurila, Eveline de Bruin, Benita5, Anaka911mail, and Sonorax.

Shutterstock: CEMX.

Wikimedia Commons: Keith Kessel.

Flickr: Smithsonian's National Zoo.

Loved all these great facts and photos? Discover MORE about your favourite pets and animals in these books:

- **I Want A Bearded Dragon**
- **I Want A Leopard Gecko**
- **I Want A Kitten**
- **I Want A Puppy**

- **Fun Leopard Gecko and Bearded Dragon Facts for Kids**
- **Fun Reptile Facts for Kids**
- **Fun Dog Facts for Kids**
- **Fun Cat Facts for Kids**
- **Fun Pony Facts for Kids**
- **Fun Horse Facts for Kids**
- **Fun Bird Facts for Kids**
- **Fun Backyard Bird Facts for Kids**
- **Fun Dinosaur Facts for Kids**
- **Fun T-Rex Facts for Kids**

www.ingramcontent.com/pod-product-compliance
Lightning Source LLC
Chambersburg PA
CBHW061202070526
44579CB00009B/100